C000089635

1,000,000 Books

are available to read at

---◆---

www.ForgottenBooks.com

---◆---

Read online
Download PDF
Purchase in print

ISBN 978-0-656-87997-7
PIBN 11112184

This book is a reproduction of an important historical work. Forgotten Books uses
state-of-the-art technology to digitally reconstruct the work, preserving the original format
whilst repairing imperfections present in the aged copy. In rare cases, an imperfection in
the original, such as a blemish or missing page, may be replicated in our edition. We do,
however, repair the vast majority of imperfections successfully; any imperfections that
remain are intentionally left to preserve the state of such historical works.

Forgotten Books is a registered trademark of FB &c Ltd.
Copyright © 2018 FB &c Ltd.
FB &c Ltd, Dalton House, 60 Windsor Avenue, London, SW19 2RR.
Company number 08720141. Registered in England and Wales.

For support please visit www.forgottenbooks.com

1 MONTH OF
FREE
READING

at

www.ForgottenBooks.com

By purchasing this book you are
eligible for one month membership to
ForgottenBooks.com, giving you
unlimited access to our entire
collection of over 1,000,000 titles via
our web site and mobile apps.

To claim your free month visit:

www.forgottenbooks.com/free1112184

* Offer is valid for 45 days from date of purchase. Terms and conditions apply.

English
Français
Deutsche
Italiano
Español
Português

www.forgottenbooks.com

Mythology Photography **Fiction**
Fishing Christianity **Art** Cooking
Essays Buddhism Freemasonry
Medicine **Biology** Music **Ancient**
Egypt Evolution Carpentry Physics
Dance Geology **Mathematics** Fitness
Shakespeare **Folklore** Yoga Marketing
Confidence Immortality Biographies
Poetry **Psychology** Witchcraft
Electronics Chemistry History **Law**
Accounting **Philosophy** Anthropology
Alchemy Drama Quantum Mechanics
Atheism Sexual Health **Ancient History**
Entrepreneurship Languages Sport
Paleontology Needlework Islam
Metaphysics Investment Archaeology
Parenting Statistics Criminology
Motivational

Historic, archived document

Do not assume content reflects current
scientific knowledge, policies, or practices.

UNITED STATES DEPARTMENT OF AGRICULTURE

BULLETIN No. 1137

Joint Contribution from the Bureaus of Plant Industry and
Entomology, in Cooperation with the Illinois, Indiana, and
Wisconsin Agricultural Experiment Stations.

Washington, D. C.   PROFESSIONAL PAPER.   March 22, 1923

SYMPTOMS OF WHEAT ROSETTE COMPARED WITH THOSE PRODUCED BY CERTAIN INSECTS.[1]

By Harold H. McKinney, *Assistant Pathologist, Office of Cereal Investigations, Bureau of Plant Industry,* and Walter H. Larrimer, *Scientific Assistant, Office of Cereal and Forage Insect Investigations, Bureau of Entomology.*

CONTENTS.

	Page.		Page.
Introduction	1	Comparison between the symptoms of wheat rosette and those caused by the wheat strawworm	6
Symptoms of wheat rosette	2		
Symptoms produced by the Hessian fly	4	Symptoms caused by the wheat stem maggot	7
Comparison between the symptoms of wheat rosette and those caused by the Hessian fly	5	Comparison between the symptoms of wheat rosette and those caused by the wheat stem maggot	7
Symptoms produced by the wheat strawworm	6	Conclusions	7
		Literature cited	8

INTRODUCTION.

Shortly after wheat rosette was brought to the attention of plant pathologists, certain workers advanced the idea that the disease was due to an infestation of the Hessian fly (*Phytophaga destructor* Say) on account of certain characters manifested by the diseased plants which resemble those of plants infested with the larvæ or puparia of this insect. Although this view was not held by entomologists who were familiar with the situation, it was considered desirable that the latter group of workers should cooperate in the investigations in order that the possibilities of an insect cause might not be overlooked.

The writers have made observations and conducted experiments with wheat rosette and also with a number of maladies of wheat caused by insects which in certain stages of their development might be confused with wheat rosette.

During 1920–21 careful observations were made on wheat plants growing in soil infested with the causal agent of wheat rosette. Three plats of Harvest Queen (white-chaffed Red Cross) wheat were sown at intervals during the fall. These plats were 5 feet

---

[1] This bulletin deals with the disease previously designated take-all and so-called take-all which occurs in Illinois and Indiana.

wide and 2 rods long. On November 11, after the adult Hessian flies had ceased to fly, determinations of the percentage of fly infestation were made in all the plats by W. B. Cartwright, of the Bureau of Entomology. In the early part of the following spring observations were made in the same plats by Dr. R. W. Webb, of the Bureau of Plant Industry, to determine the percentage of rosette infestation. The results of these observations of infestation are given in Table 1.

TABLE 1.—*Infestations of Harvest Queen wheat by the Hessian fly in the fall of 1920 and by rosette in the spring of 1921 on plats near Granite City, Ill.*

Date of sowing.	Plants showing infestation (per cent).	
	Hessian fly, in the fall.	Rosette, in the spring.
September 21	2.5	93.6
October 4	0	85.6
October 11	0	96.0

Since rosette develops very early in the spring, before the spring emergence of the Hessian fly adults, it is obvious that any possible connection between this insect and rosette can involve only the fall infestation of the Hessian fly. It will be noted from Table 1 that there is no direct correlation between the percentage of fall Hessian fly infestation in any of the plats and the percentage of rosette in the same plats the following spring. The fall fly infestation was insignificant or absent, while the percentages of rosette were very high. It is therefore quite evident that some other factor than the Hessian fly is the prime cause of wheat rosette.

While all evidence indicates that the disease in question is not caused by an insect, particularly the Hessian fly, it is recognized that under certain conditions there is a possibility of confusing the symptoms of the disease with certain of those produced by the Hessian fly, the wheat strawworm (*Harmolita grandis* Riley), and to a less extent the wheat stem maggot (*Meromyza americana* Fitch). It therefore seems advisable to give the chief points of similarity and difference between the symptoms of the maladies under discussion.

The insects discussed in this paper have long been recognized as important wheat pests, and details of their respective life histories will not be included. Osborn (*2*),[2] Webster (*5*), and many others have recorded the life history of the Hessian fly. Phillips (*3*) has given similar information concerning the wheat strawworm, and Webster (*4*) has discussed the life history of the wheat stem maggot.

SYMPTOMS OF WHEAT ROSETTE.

A complete description of the symptoms of wheat rosette has been given by the senior writer in another publication (*1*).

FALL PERIOD.

Field symptoms.—As this disease is interpreted at the present time there are apparently no field symptoms in the fall. During the past two seasons a highly susceptible variety of wheat growing

---

[2] Serial numbers (italic) in parentheses refer to "Literature cited" on page 8 of this bulletin.

on soil of extremely high infestation appeared to be in a perfect state of health during the autumn. While certain fungi infect the outer tissues of the subterranean tiller parts and the subcrown internode,[3] the general field appearance of the plants was far better than that of varieties not known to develop wheat rosette.

Plant symptoms.—While the characteristic plant symptoms of the disease do not develop in the fall, close observations and tiller counts seem to indicate that the excessive development of tillers, which is so characteristic of the disease in the spring, commences to a certain extent in the autumn. However, since other important symptoms are not associated with this fall condition, its importance as a fall symptom and as an indicator of the development of the disease in the spring is still a question.

SPRING PERIOD.

Field symptoms.—The first positive indications of the disease become evident early in the spring after the growth of the healthy plants is well started. In the fields but slightly infested, distinct patches of badly dwarfed plants show here and there without regard to the type or condition of the soil (Pl. I). Such patches may vary in size from those containing but a few diseased plants to areas many feet in diameter. Often these patches are almost circular in shape, while others are irregular. It is not uncommon to find diseased plants occurring singly intermixed with healthy plants. In cases where spotting occurs, the edges of such spots are usually more sharply defined than the margins of spots caused by unfavorable soil conditions, especially poor drainage. In the rosette-spotted areas most of the plants are diseased and therefore stunted right up to the edge of the spot. In spots caused by local unfavorable soil conditions all the plants usually decrease in height gradually from the edge toward the center.

In fields more severely infested it is not uncommon to find a large proportion or in some cases all of the field involved. In such cases most of the plants may be affected. There is no case on record, however, where all plants in a large area have developed the disease. Investigations have shown that apparently there are resistant strains in the most susceptible varieties.

A striking characteristic of fields affected by the disease in the early spring is the comparative freedom from blank spaces or areas due to dead plants. Practically all plants are intact, even though diseased. Later in the spring, however, under certain conditions such plants may die. During seasons of heavy rainfall diseased plants may be washed out of the soil, causing blank areas in the field, but this condition is rather unusual.

Plant symptoms.—Plants affected by rosette remain dormant in the spring after healthy plants commence their spring growth. The fall tillers of the diseased plants usually do not " shoot," or if they do the process is delayed and of short duration. The leaves of diseased plants are dark blue-green in color. They are rather broad and stiff. Thus far no parasites or external lesions have been found consistently associated with the vital tissues of diseased plants during this period.

---

[3] The term subcrown internode is used to designate the elongated region which under certain conditions develops between the seed and the crown of the plant.

A little later in the spring an excessive number of tillers becomes strikingly evident, giving the diseased plants a rosette appearance (Pl. II, *B*). Later, the underground portion of the older tillers develops a brown, rotted condition (Pl. I, *C*).

SUMMER PERIOD.

Field symptoms.—In case of badly infested wheat fields, those plants which escape or resist rosette develop and form a thin stand of grain, and the diseased plants under usual conditions slowly recover by sending up straggling secondary tillers. In the case of the early death of diseased plants, the thick tufts of plant remains will be found on the ground usually until after harvest, except during seasons of heavy rainfall, when these plants are practically all washed away.

Recovering diseased plants do not ripen until after the healthy plants; hence, as the healthy plants turn in color at maturity the diseased areas show up conspicuously as green spots in the ripening, healthy grain.

Plant symptoms.—In the case of diseased plants which do not recover, their dead remains, consisting of low compact tufts of tillers and leaves, will be found in place on the ground except where they have been washed away. Plants which recover consist of a number of straggling secondary culms coming up from the stool of dead fall tillers and leaves. Such secondary culms may or may not produce heads. In some cases remarkable recovery occurs, especially on rich moist soil, but usually very small imperfectly filled heads develop. Frequently, plants are found in which only part of the tillers are diseased. In such cases the healthy tillers usually develop normally, resulting in a plant consisting of a few normal tillers with dead fall tillers at the base and perhaps a few secondary tillers attempting to attain maturity.

SYMPTOMS PRODUCED BY THE HESSIAN FLY.

FALL PERIOD.

Field symptoms.—A wheat field infested with the Hessian fly is of a shade of green darker than normal, with a certain bristling appearance due to the stiff and upright leaves of the infested plants. As the season advances, the seemingly healthy appearance gives way to a more or less ragged, sickly stage, described by the farmer as "going back."

Under certain conditions seemingly dependent upon the response of the wheat plant to soil variations, there may be a decided field spotting due to fly infestation. These spots or patches are usually associated with such conditions as soil color, type, topography, and exposure.

Plant symptoms.—In the case of an infested plant, the central shoot is usually absent, and the leaves are broad, short, more or less stiff, and of a dark-green color (Pl. II, *E*). By stripping down the leaf sheath, the larva or the puparium (flaxseed) can easily be found near the base of the plant (Pl. III, *E*). The presence of a single small larva or a flaxseed is sufficient to have caused the characteristic appearance of the wheat plant. An infested plant may produce a few normal tillers or it may be killed, depending upon the degree of infestation. In the latter case, as the season advances the plant

SYMPTOMS OF WHEAT ROSETTE.

A typical spot in a field caused by the rosette of wheat. Note the dwarf and leafy appearance of the diseased plants in the lower right-hand portion of the picture as compared with the surrounding tall, healthy plants.

PLATE II.

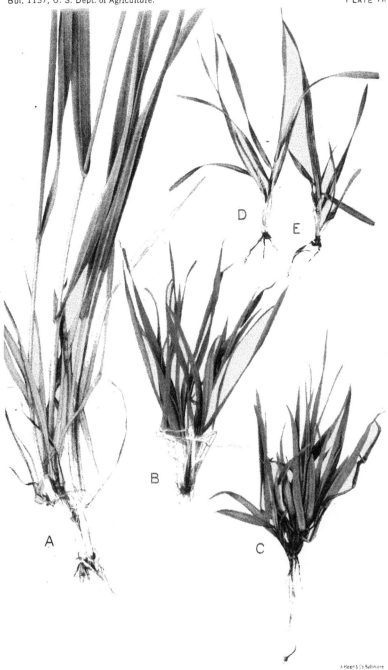

A Hoen & Co Baltimore

PLANTS OF WINTER WHEAT SHOWING THE EFFECTS OF ATTACKS OF THE ROSETTE
AND THE HESSIAN FLY, RESPECTIVELY, COMPARED WITH HEALTHY PLANTS.

A, Healthy plant in the spring; B and C, plants of the same age as A, showing early and
advanced stages, respectively, of the rosette; D, healthy plant as it appears in the late
autumn; E, plant of the same age as D, infested by the Hessian fly. Note the similarities
in color but the differences in the extent of tillering in plants affected by the two maladies
compared with the corresponding healthy plants.

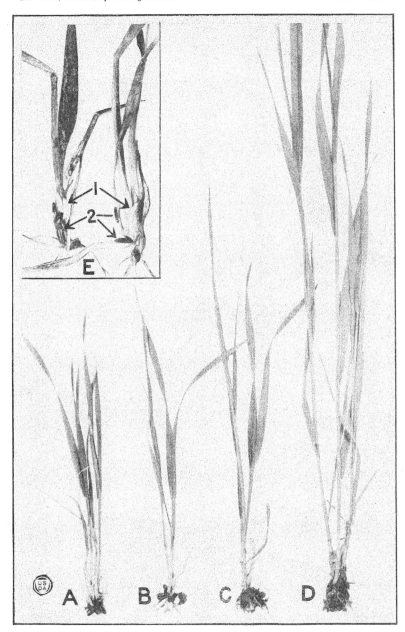

WHEAT PLANTS INFESTED BY THE HESSIAN FLY COMPARED WITH AN UNINFESTED PLANT.

A, *B*, and *C*, Spring-wheat plants infested by the Hessian fly; *D*, healthy plant of the same age for comparison. The infested plants are much dwarfed and show the same dark-green color in comparison with the healthy plant as is shown in Plate II, *D* and *E*. *E*, Winter-wheat plants infested by the Hessian fly, showing larvæ (1) and puparia (2) (flaxseeds) of the insect. The leaf sheaths have been stripped away.

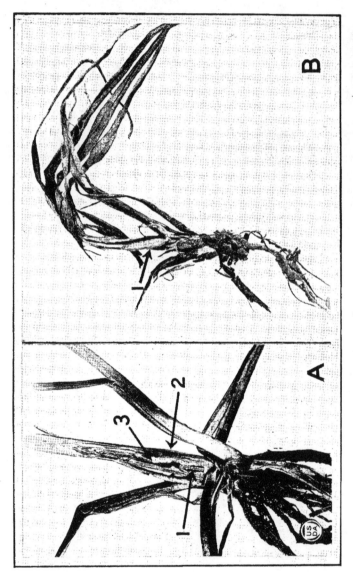

PLANTS OF WINTER WHEAT INFESTED BY THE WHEAT STRAWWORM AND THE WHEAT STEM MAGGOT.

A, An infested winter-wheat plant early in the spring, showing the larva (1) of the wheat strawworm (*Harmolita grandis* Riley). Note the rather elongated, bulblike swelling (2) and the cavity (3) in the infested tiller. *B*, An infested winter-wheat plant early in the spring, killed by the attacks of the larva (1) of the wheat stem maggot (*Meromyza americana* Fitch).

rapidly decays, leaving the flaxseeds more or less free in or on the surface of the soil. This condition persists until the emergence of the principal spring brood of the fly.

SPRING PERIOD.

Field symptoms.—In the case of extremely heavy infestation the previous fall, practically all the plants may be killed. Varying degrees of infestation give the field a more or less ragged, bunchy appearance, and numerous blank spaces or areas may be evident. As the principal spring generation begins to get in its work, the general color of the field becomes a dark green, and growth is retarded in accordance with the severity of the infestation.

Plant symptoms.—The effect of infestation on small plants in the spring is practically the same as in the fall, and larvæ and flaxseeds are located at relatively the same place on the culms. On larger plants the larvæ or the flaxseeds may be found higher up on the stem, but they may easily be found by stripping down the leaf sheath. The culm may be killed or not, depending on its size and the number of larvæ or flaxseeds present.

SUMMER PERIOD.

Field symptoms.—A thin stand with fallen straw, depending on the severity of the infestation, usually marks an infested field in summer. A light infestation may escape notice.

Plant symptoms.—Culms that have become weakened at the location of the flaxseeds usually fall over before harvest. Culms that were heavily infested may have been killed or prevented from producing a head, but in any case the flaxseeds may be found as the cause.

COMPARISON BETWEEN THE SYMPTOMS OF WHEAT ROSETTE AND THOSE CAUSED BY THE HESSIAN FLY.

Since rosette is not apparent in the autumn and since it becomes evident in the spring before the emergence of the adult Hessian fly, there is very little chance to confuse the two maladies during these periods.

In the late spring there is a possibility of confusion, especially if plants affected by rosette show, in addition, the spring infestation of the Hessian fly.

In the latter part of the spring, fields affected by rosette sometimes show blank areas caused by the diseased plants being washed out of the soil by unusually heavy rains. Such fields are practically indistinguishable from those suffering from a severe attack of the fly, when the infestation of either is general over the field. Owing to the fact, however, that spring fly infestation has never been noted to occur in localized areas or spots in the field, as is commonly the case with wheat rosette, such field spotting observed at any time during the growing season practically precludes fly injury as the sole cause, even though all the affected plants may have been washed away.

In the case of plant symptoms, fly infestation causes a reduction rather than an increased number of tillers, as is the case in plants affected by rosette. While plants affected by the latter malady often show fly infestation, it will usually be found that many near-by plants affected by rosette show no evidence of such infestation. In the case of plants suffering from fly injury, the larva or flaxseed of the insect or the empty flaxseeds will be found at the base of the plant, usually under the first leaf sheath.

SYMPTOMS PRODUCED BY THE WHEAT STRAWWORM.

FALL PERIOD.

The wheat strawworm passes the fall and winter in the old stubble or straw, so of course it has no effect upon the fall growth of winter wheat.

SPRING PERIOD.

Field symptoms.—Almost invariably the infestation by the wheat strawworm occurs in a field bordering on old stubble or in a field which the previous year was in wheat the stubble of which was poorly plowed. In the first case the stand is thinner and plants shorter next to the old stubble field, and this difference gradually shades off to normal as the distance from the edge of the field increases. This is due to the inability of the wingless form of the insect to travel far, and for this reason most of the infestation occurs within a strip 30 yards wide bordering on the old stubble.

Plant symptoms.—Plants infested by the strawworm resemble those infested by the Hessian fly except that in the former case tillering up to this time has been normal. The larvæ develop at the base of the plant, causing a bulblike swelling to appear at that point. The infested culms are always killed, and frequently all the culms are infested. The swelling usually serves to identify the injury caused by this insect, and of course the larvæ or pupæ of the insect itself (Pl. IV, *A*) are inside the stem, while in the case of the Hessian fly the larva or flaxseed is merely under the leaf sheath.

SUMMER PERIOD.

Field symptoms.—The thin stand along the old stubble field is all that serves to mark an infested field in summer. The second generation of the insect has enabled it to spread throughout the whole field.

Plant symptoms.—The decaying remains of tillers infested earlier in the season are about all that marks the plants which have been infested. The larval form of the second generation in the straw at this time is difficult to locate except by splitting the infested straw.

COMPARISON BETWEEN THE SYMPTOMS OF WHEAT ROSETTE AND THOSE CAUSED BY THE WHEAT STRAWWORM.

Wheat rosette is not confined to the vicinity of old wheat stubble fields, as is the case with the strawworm infestation. If the former malady occurs near such a stubble field its presence can be distinguished by means of the bulblike swelling on plants infested with the insect; also the latter plants develop the normal number of tillers in contrast with the excessive tillering caused by rosette. The dead and decayed culms in late spring or autumn killed by the first generation of the strawworm will still be recognizable by their bulbous growth containing the refuse left by the larvæ of this generation.

SYMPTOMS CAUSED BY THE WHEAT STEM MAGGOT.

FALL PERIOD.

Field symptoms.—A field infested by the wheat stem maggot has very much the same appearance as if infested by the Hessian fly. The stem maggot is not usually so prevalent as the fly, and instances of extreme infestation are more rare. The color of an infested field is a darker green than normal, and when severely infested the ragged, sickly appearance comes on earlier than if infested by the Hessian fly.

Plant symptoms.—An infested plant has the center shoot discolored or dead and the other leaves broader and darker green than normal. The larva, difficult to find when small, occurs at the base of the stem, where it lacerates the tender tissues with its mouth hooks and feeds upon the juices.

SPRING PERIOD.

Field symptoms.—Depending upon the severity of the infestation, gaps in the drill row caused by the dead plants mark a field infested by the wheat stem maggot in spring; but there are so many other causes of this same appearance that it can not be taken as characteristic of this insect.

Plant symptoms.—The infested culms, and frequently the entire plant, if able to withstand the injury during the fall, usually die during the winter. Therefore, in the spring these dead and more or less disintegrated plants contain the full-grown larvæ or pupæ of the insect (Pl. IV, *B*).

COMPARISON BETWEEN THE SYMPTOMS OF WHEAT ROSETTE AND THOSE CAUSED BY THE WHEAT STEM MAGGOT.

As in the case of the fall infestation of the Hessian fly, the symptoms produced by an infestation of wheat stem maggot in the autumn will not lead to confusion with rosette, even though the plants affected by the two maladies resemble each other in certain respects. There is practically no chance for confusing the troubles in the spring, because the spring infestation of the maggot does not cause symptoms which resemble the fall symptoms in any way.

CONCLUSIONS.

The insect injuries described in this bulletin may usually be diagnosed with certainty, on account of the presence in some stage of the insect on the affected plant. However, in the late stages of these disorders it is sometimes difficult to find any trace of the insect, and in such cases the infested fields and affected plants are difficult or impossible to distinguish from fields and plants affected by rosette.

The symptoms of rosette can not be distinguished with certainty after the spring period, and it is safer not to diagnose the disease positively after early spring, especially if heavy rains have washed out many diseased plants.

In the early spring the disease manifests itself by a retarded development of the plants, followed by excessive tillering and a dark blue-green coloration, the leaves being broad and stiff and the whole plant having a bunchy rosette appearance. At this time, when the disease is not complicated with insect infestations the drill rows do not have any blank spaces.

LITERATURE CITED.

(1) McKinney, H. H.
　　　1923. Investigations on the rosette disease of wheat and its control.
　　　　　In Jour. Agr. Research, v. 23, no. 10. [In press.]

(2) Osborn, Herbert.
　　　1898. The Hessian fly in the United States. U. S. Dept. Agr., Div.
　　　　　Ent. Bul. 16, n. s., 58 p., 8 fig., front., 2 pl. Bibliography, p. 48–57.

(3) Phillips, W.-J.
　　　1920. Studies on the life history and habits of the jointworm flies of
　　　　　the genus Harmolita (Isosoma), with recommendations for control.
　　　　　U. S. Dept. Agr. Bul. 808, 27 p., 8 fig., 6 pl.

(4) Webster, F. M.
　　　1903. Some insects attacking the stems of growing wheat, rye, barley,
　　　　　and oats. U. S. Dept. Agr., Div. Ent. Bul. 42, 62 p., 15 fig.

(5)　　　1920. The Hessian fly and how to prevent losses from it. U. S. Dept.
　　　　　Agr., Farmers' Bul. 1083, 16 p., 13 fig.

ORGANIZATION OF THE UNITED STATES DEPARTMENT OF AGRICULTURE.

Secretary of Agriculture _____ Henry C. Wallace.
Assistant Secretary _____ C. W. Pugsley.
Director of Scientific Work _____ E. D. Ball.
Director of Regulatory Work _____
Weather Bureau _____ Charles F. Marvin, *Chief.*
Bureau of Agricultural Economics _____ Henry C. Taylor, *Chief.*
Bureau of Animal Industry _____ John R. Mohler, *Chief.*
Bureau of Plant Industry _____ William A. Taylor, *Chief.*
Forest Service _____ W. B. Greeley, *Chief.*
Bureau of Chemistry _____ Walter G. Campbell, *Acting Chief.*
Bureau of Soils _____ Milton Whitney, *Chief.*
Bureau of Entomology _____ L. O. Howard, *Chief.*
Bureau of Biological Survey _____ E. W. Nelson, *Chief.*
Bureau of Public Roads _____ Thomas H. MacDonald, *Chief.*
Fixed Nitrogen Research Laboratory _____ F. G. Cottrell, *Director.*
Division of Accounts and Disbursements _____ A. Zappone, *Chief.*
Division of Publications _____ John L. Cobbs, Jr., *Chief.*
Library _____ Claribel R. Barnett, *Librarian.*
States Relations Service _____ A. C. True, *Director.*
Federal Horticultural Board _____ C. L. Marlatt, *Chairman.*
Insecticide and Fungicide Board _____ J. K. Haywood, *Chairman.*
Packers and Stockyards Administration _____ ⎫Chester Morrill, *Assistant to the*
Grain Future Trading Act Administration ____ ⎭　*Secretary.*
Office of the Solicitor _____ R. W. Williams, *Solicitor.*

This bulletin is a contribution from the—

Bureau of Plant Industry _____ William A. Taylor, *Chief.*
　Office of Cereal Investigations _____ Carleton R. Ball, *Cerealist in
　　　　　　　　　　　　　　　　　　　　　　　　　　　　Charge.*
Bureau of Entomology _____ L. O. Howard, *Chief.*
　Office of Cereal and Forage Insect In-
　　vestigations _____ W. R. Walton, *Entomologist in
　　　　　　　　　　　　　　　　　　　　　　　　　　　　Charge.*

CPSIA information can be obtained
at www.ICGtesting.com
Printed in the USA
LVHW081445211118
597922LV00010B/553/P